Adorable Kittens
A Grayscale Coloring Book for Adults

Dar Payment

The Amazing Grayscale Coloring Company
Lake Elsinore, CA USA

Book design and cover art
By Dar Payment

Photographs sourced from Pixabay and PublicDomainPictures.net

Copyright © 2017 by Dar Payment

All rights reserved. No part of this book may be reproduced, stored in a retrieval system or transmitted, in any form or by any means, electronic, mechanical, photocopying, recording or otherwise, without the prior written consent from the author.

ISBN-13: 978-1976433078

Published by:

The Amazing Grayscale Coloring Company
A Division of DAP Publishing
Lake Elsinore, California USA

www.AmazingGrayscale.com

A Note from the Author

It was not my original intention to put together a coloring book. I am not a professional artist, but I love to color grayscale! And to be honest, the grayscale coloring selection I have shared with you in the following pages of this book are from one of my own private collections.

About a year ago I became totally fascinated with every aspect of coloring – especially with projects concerning grayscale. I was so excited that I began to host small coloring parties with my friends, offering many of the grayscale pages appearing in this book for our coloring inspirations.

My friends loved the coloring projects. Soon they were hooked and told me they wanted more similar grayscale pages to color!

These friends would often show their finished coloring projects with their friends, who wanted to color too . . . and well, the rest is joyful providence. The cumulation of the grayscale coloring book you are now holding in your hands.

Have fun bringing the images to life by filling them up with tons of beautiful color. And if you become obsessed with coloring like I did (and still am) and want to spread the love of coloring with your friends too, host your own coloring party using the pages of this book!

Blessings and Happy Coloring,

Dar Payment

"I prefer living in color." ~ David Hockney

How to Color Grayscale

Coloring grayscale is very easy, and there are a few schools of thought out there about how to color a grayscale image or photograph.

The number one thing about coloring grayscale is that the shading is already there for you which means no more trying to figure out where your light source or shadows need to be, etc..

The first grayscale coloring method is to use one color over each area first using very light pressure over the entire area you wish to color. Next, using the same color apply heavier pressure in the darker shaded areas.

Another method is to simply use your darkest colors to color over the areas with the heaviest gray shading. Then your lighter colors over the areas with the lightest gray shading, and finally using your medium colors to blend both the light and dark colors.

The point is that there is no wrong or right way to color grayscale. So have fun experimenting as you unleash your inner colorist, and enjoy watching as your photo or image comes to life before your eyes.

Need samples of coloring inspirations for the images in this book? Download a free full colored template containing all of the coloring inspirations depicted in this book at: https://www.amazinggrayscale.com/Free-Downloads.php

The Best Artist Mediums for This Book

The best artist mediums for this book are colored pencils. You can experiment with gel pens and markers if you'd like, but gel pens and markers will bleed through the page.

If you do choose to use gel pens or markers the best practice is to put a piece of paper underneath your coloring project in order to protect from bleed through onto the coloring page underneath it.

"Kittens are angels with whiskers."
~Terri Guillemets

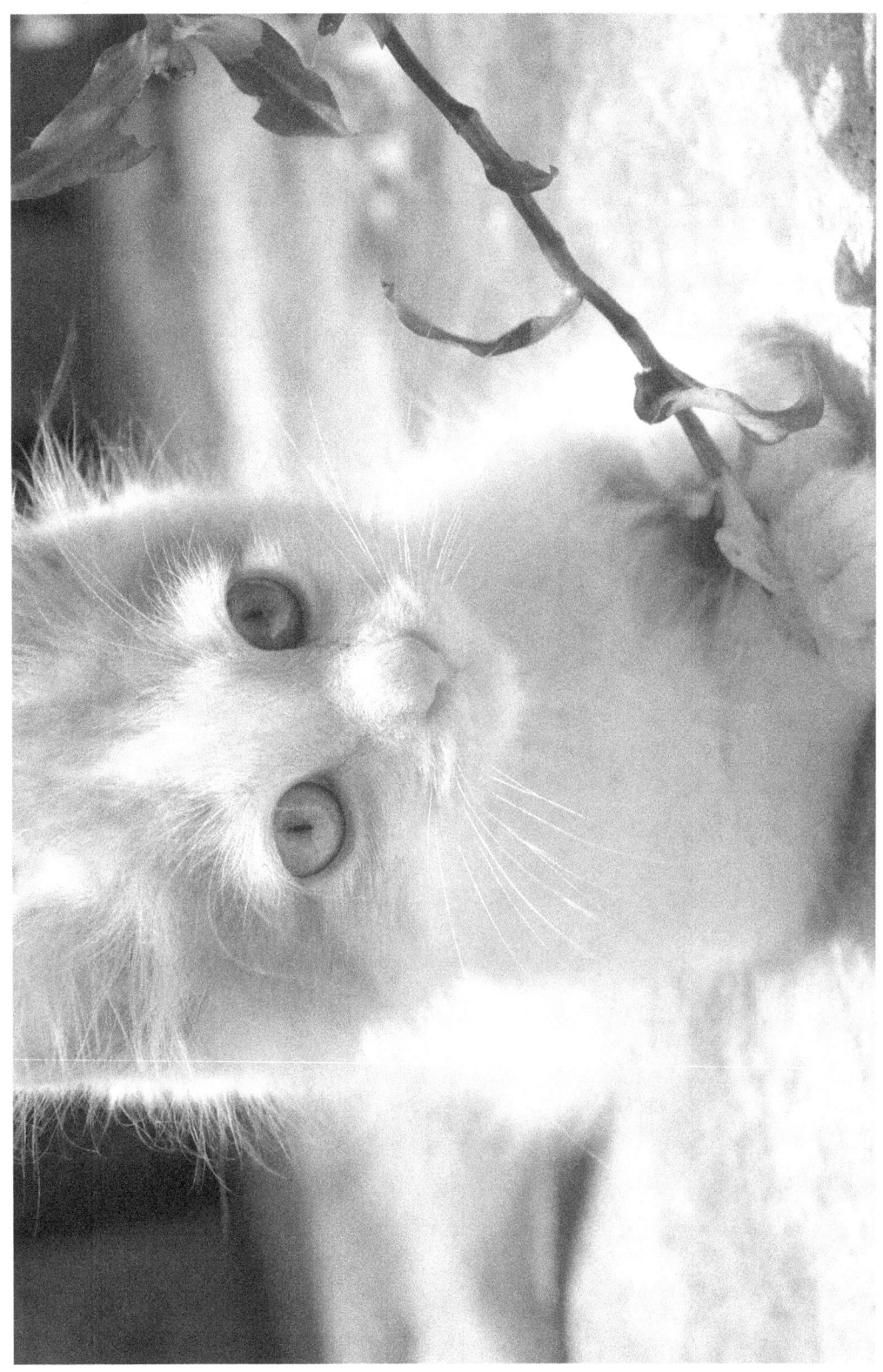

*"A kitten is, in the animal world,
what a rosebud is in the garden."*
~ Robert Sowthey

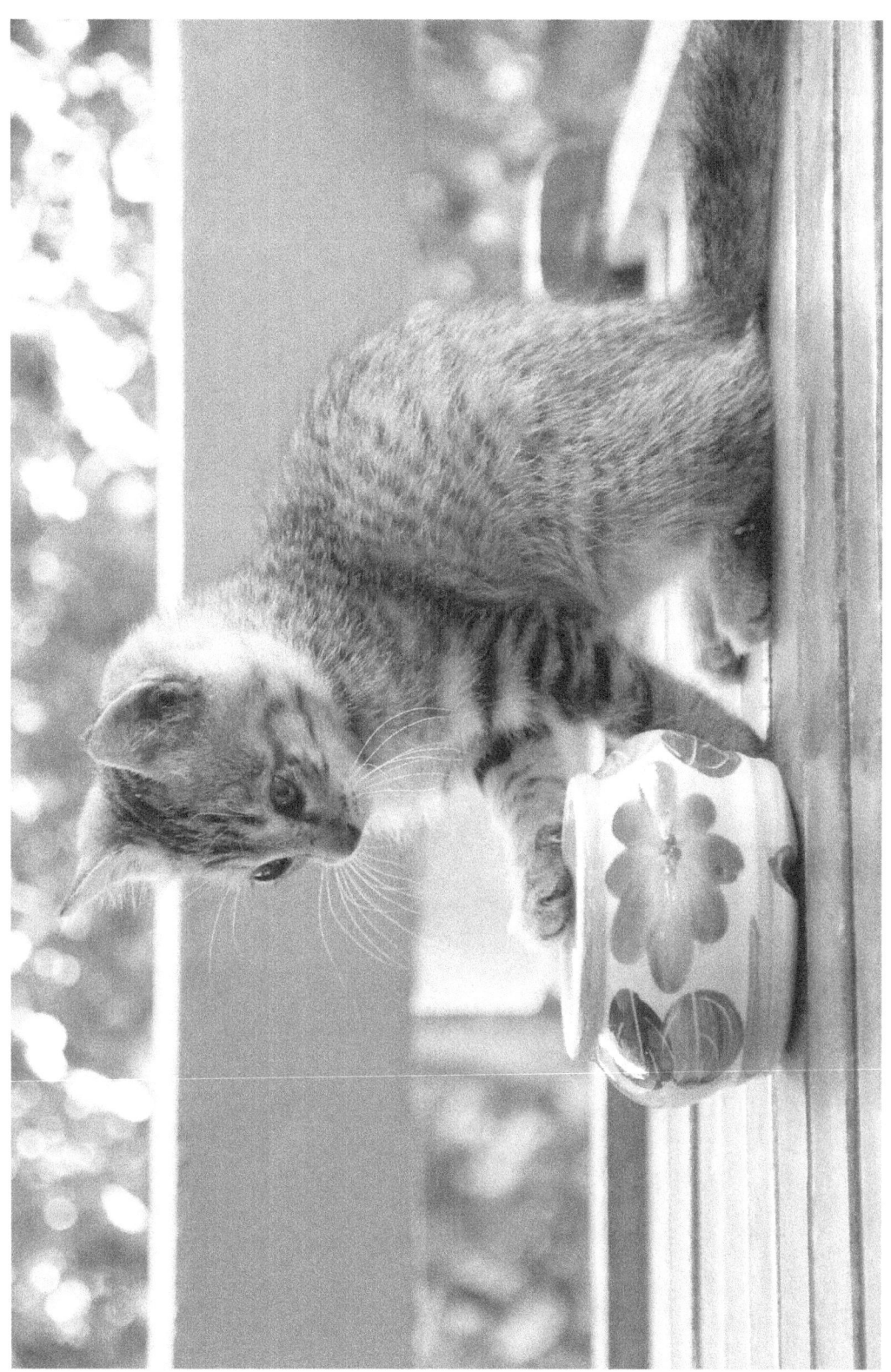

"A kitten is the delight of a household. All day long a comedy is played out by an incomparable actor."
~ Jules Champfleury

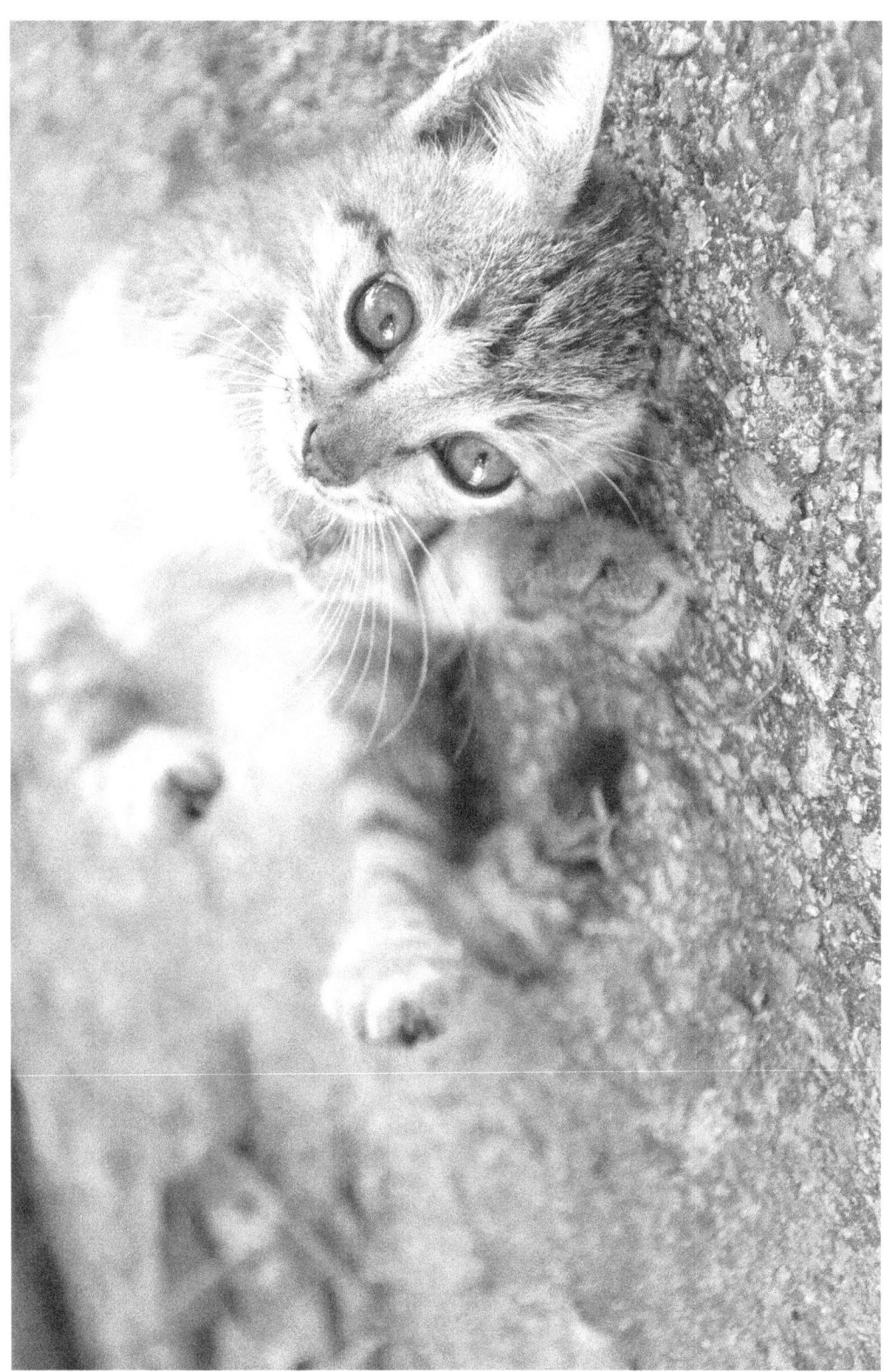

*"for those memories are now
just like these little kittens
I hold in my hands
those can be kissed
and treasured
but not held too tightly."
~ Sanober Khan*

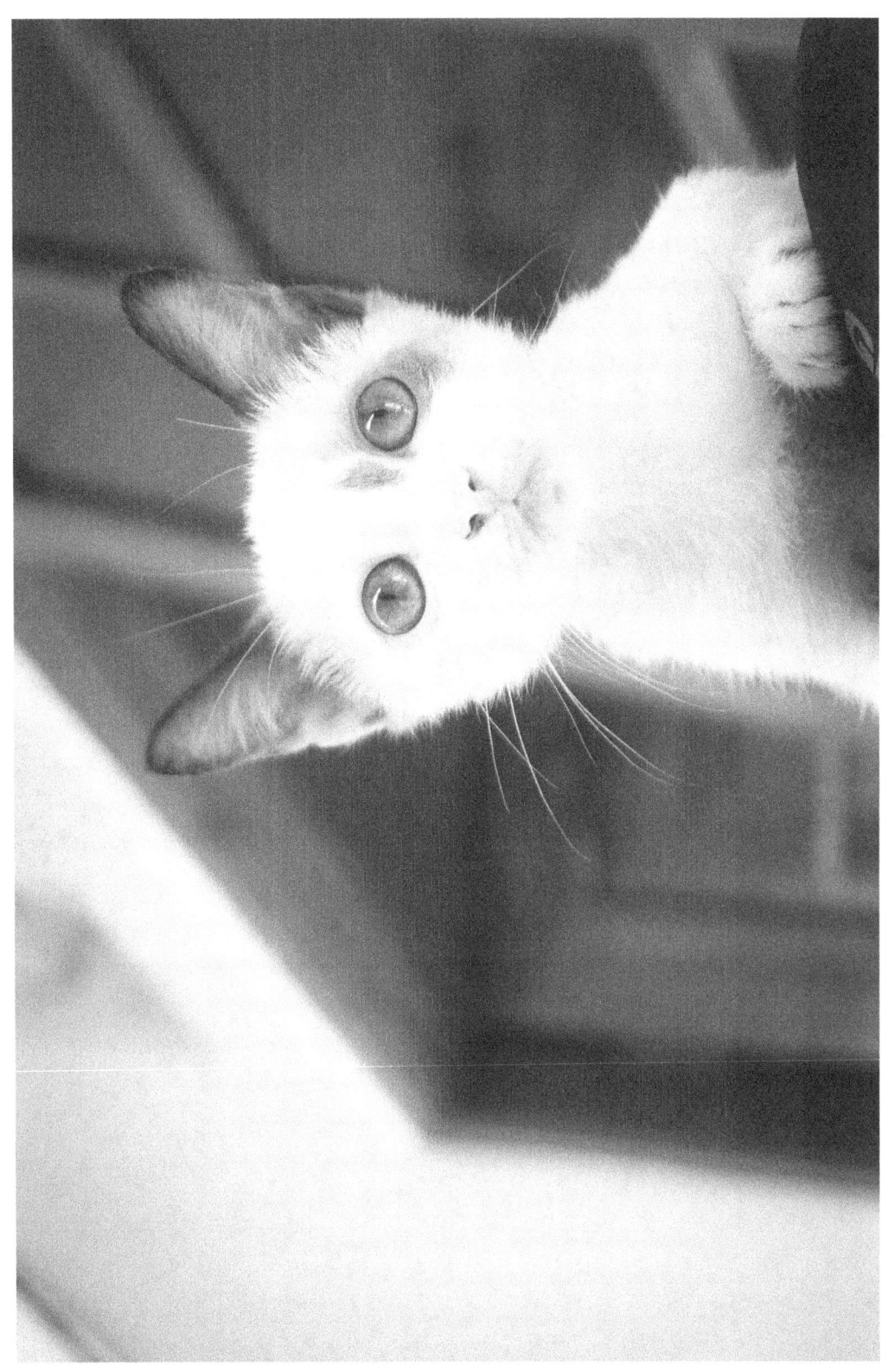

"The only thing a cat worries about is what's happening right now. As we tell the kittens, you can only wash one paw at a time."
~ Lloyd Alexander

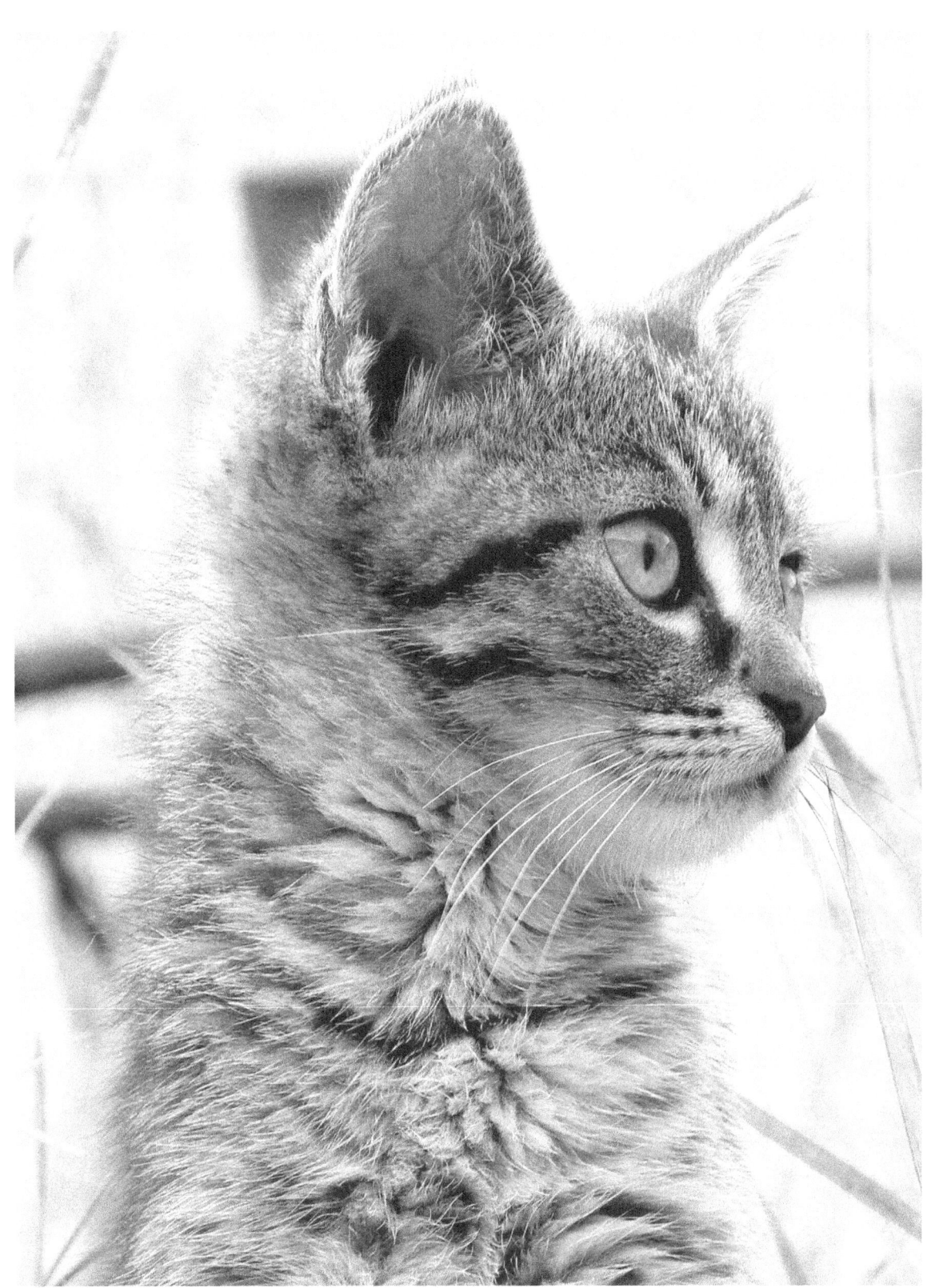

"Poems are soft kitten furs. smoothing out the rough edges of my world."
~ Sanober Khan

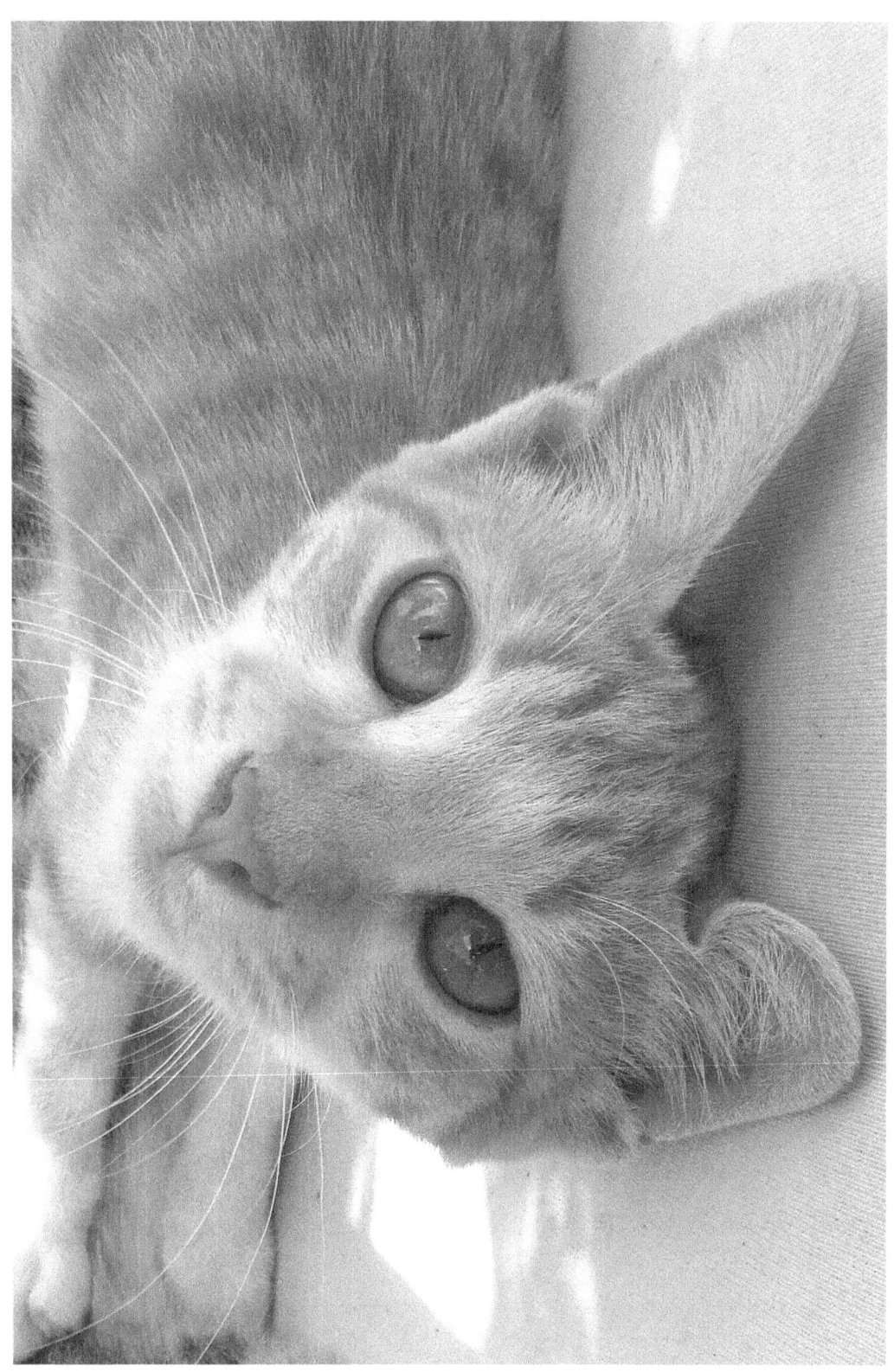

"A kitten gets himself into every kind of trouble."
~ Jules Champfleury

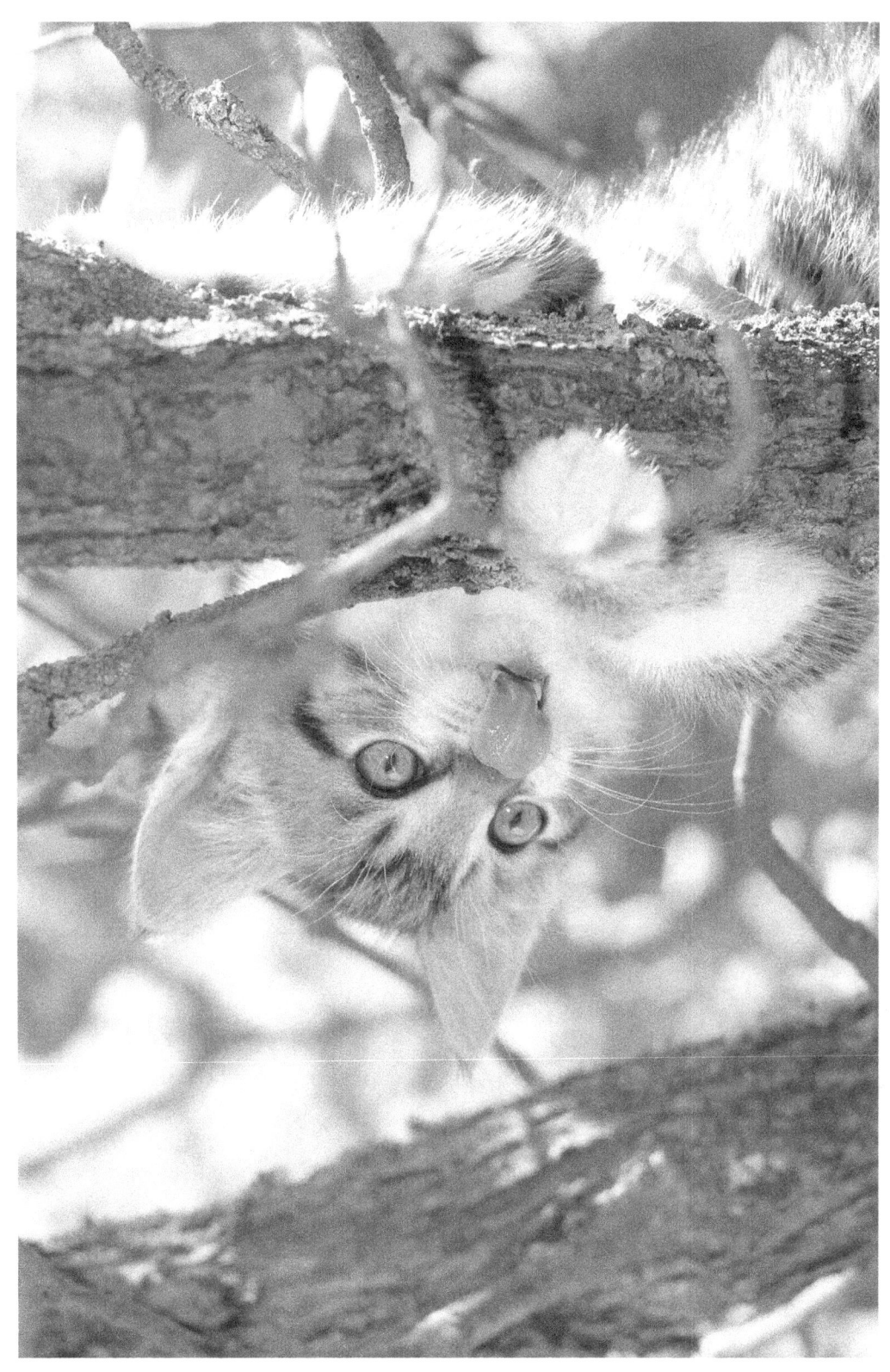

"What feeling is so nice as a child's hand in yours? So small, so soft and warm, than a kitten huddling in the shelter of your clasp?"
~ Wilson Mizner

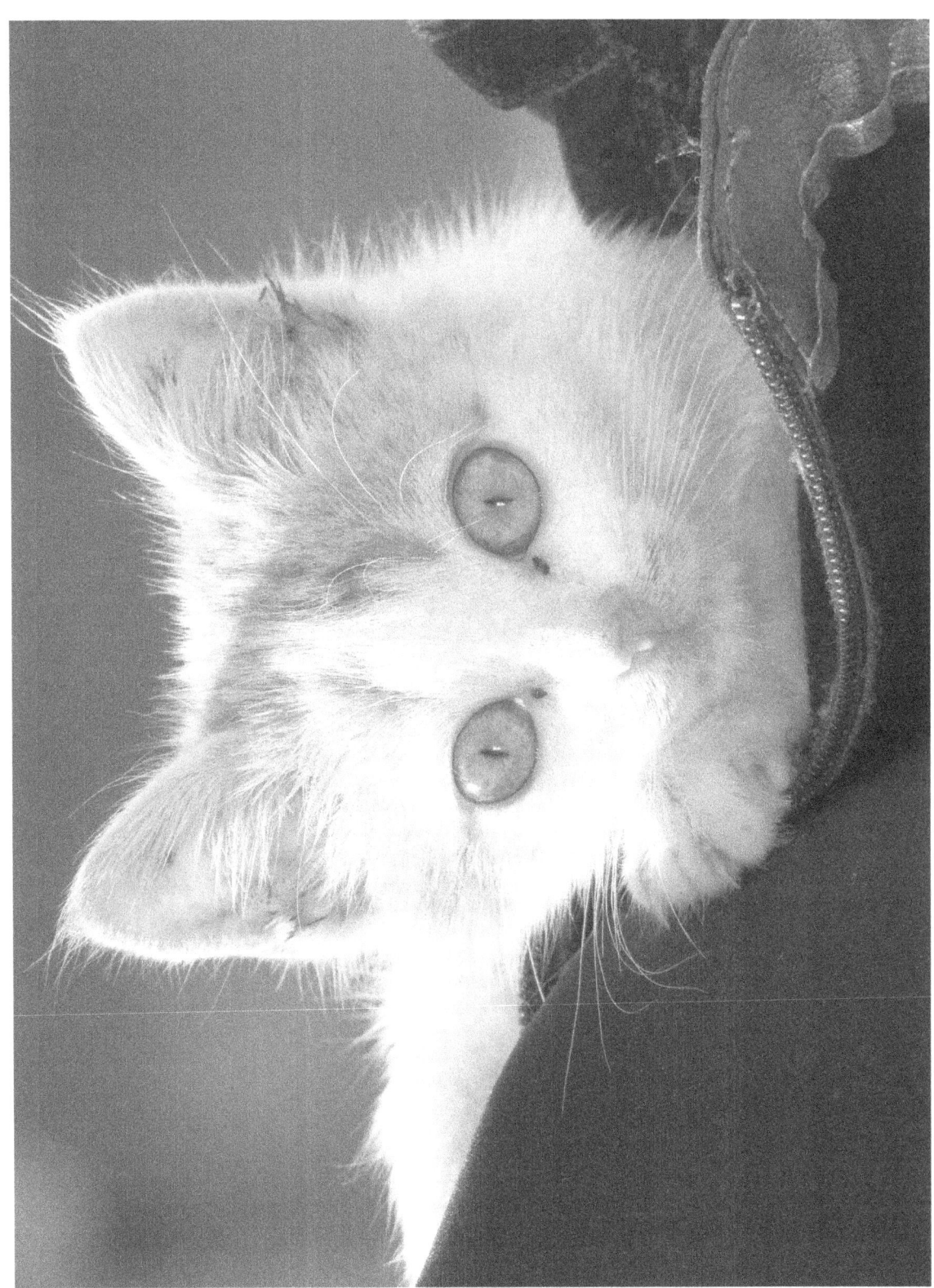

"Kittens believe that all nature is occupied with their diversion."
~ F.A. Paradis de Moncrif

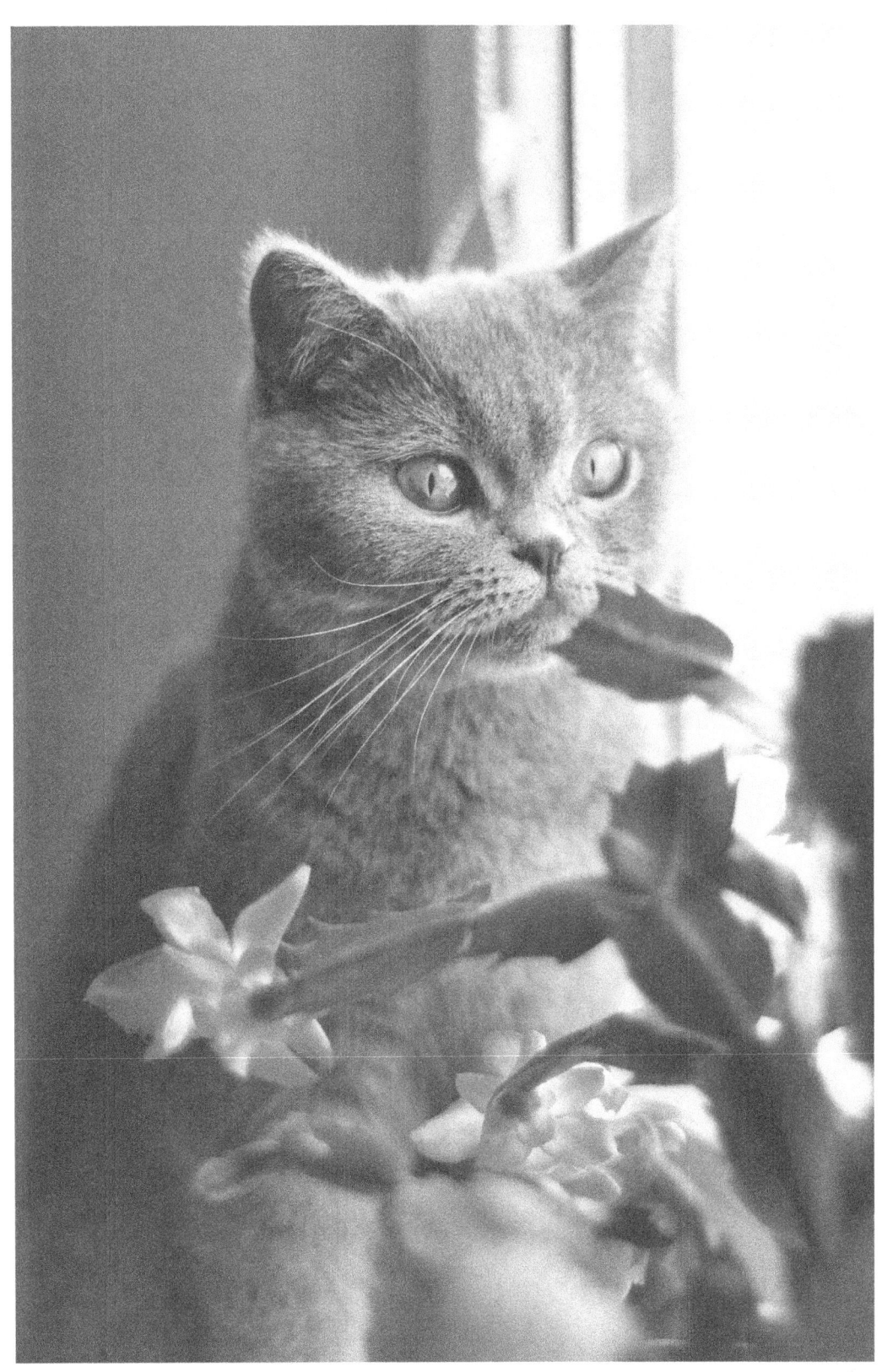

"Kitten, four hours of sleep while holding you is far more beneficial to me than eight hours of endless tossing and turning because you're not there."
~ Jeaniene Frost

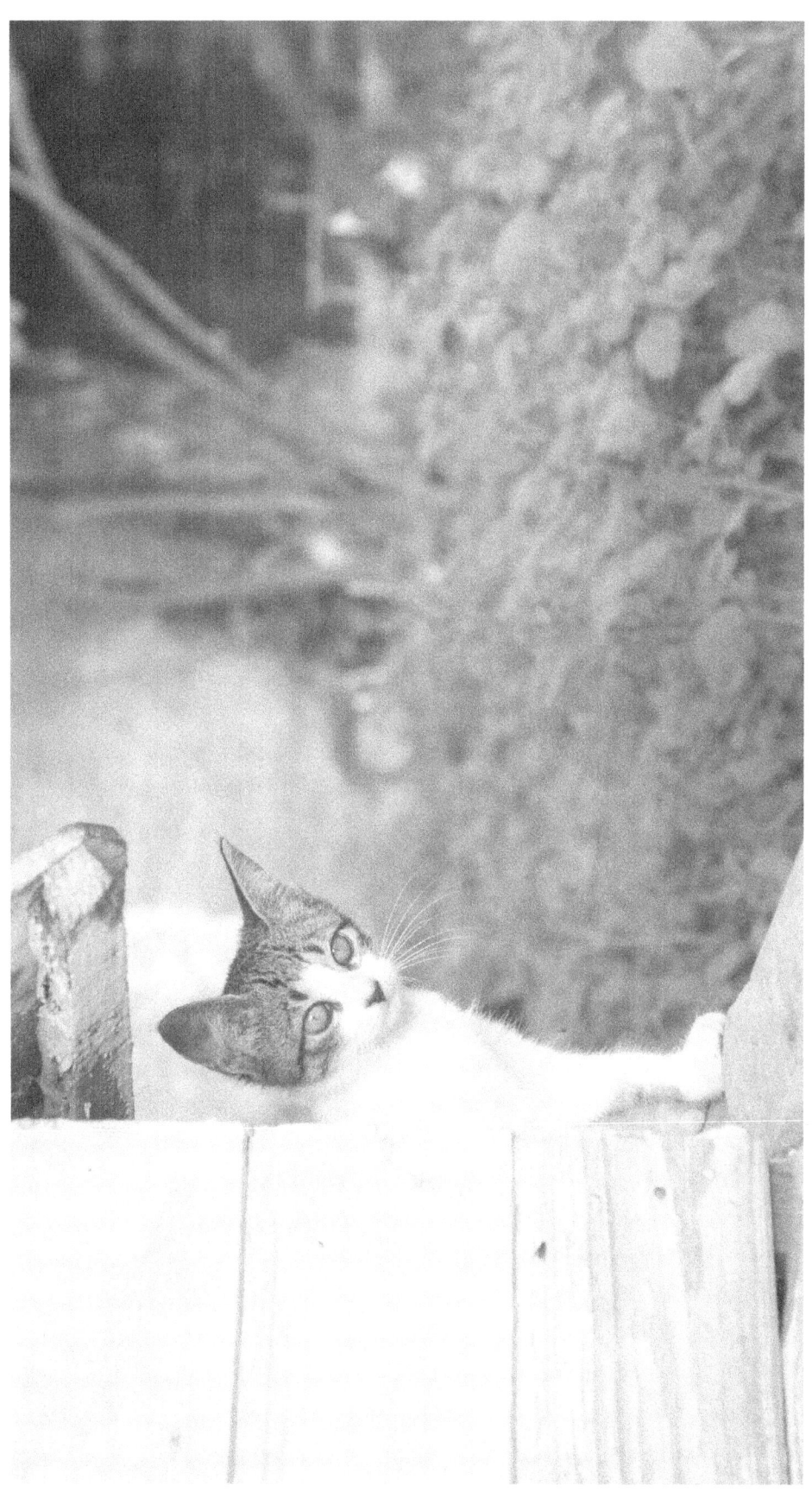

"Kittens will make your sad go away."
~ David Wong

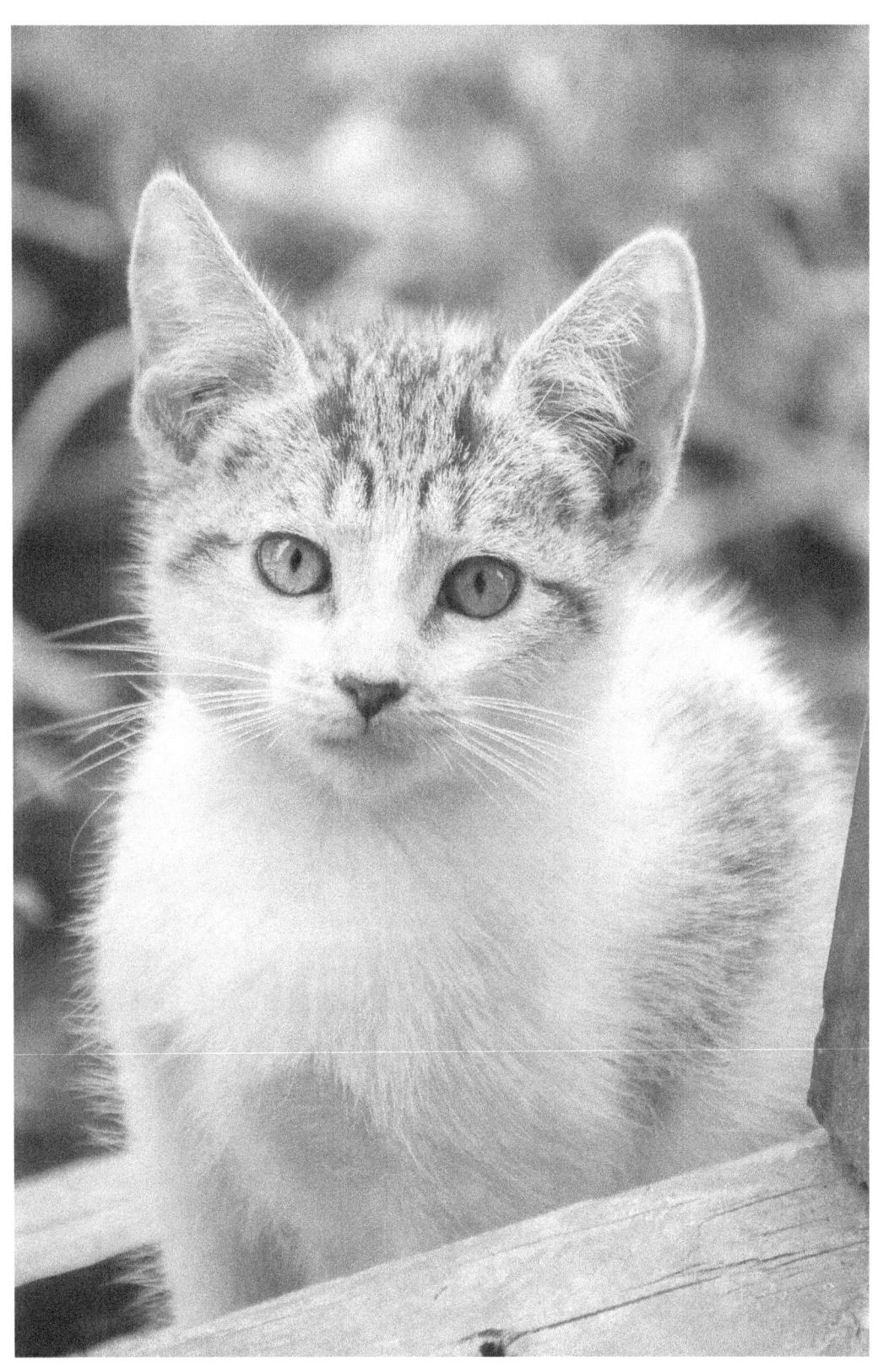

"A kitten is the most irresistible comedian in the world. Its wide-open eyes gleam with wonder and mirth. It darts madly at nothing at all, and then, as though suddenly checked in the pursuit, prances sideways . . . "
~ Agnes Repplier

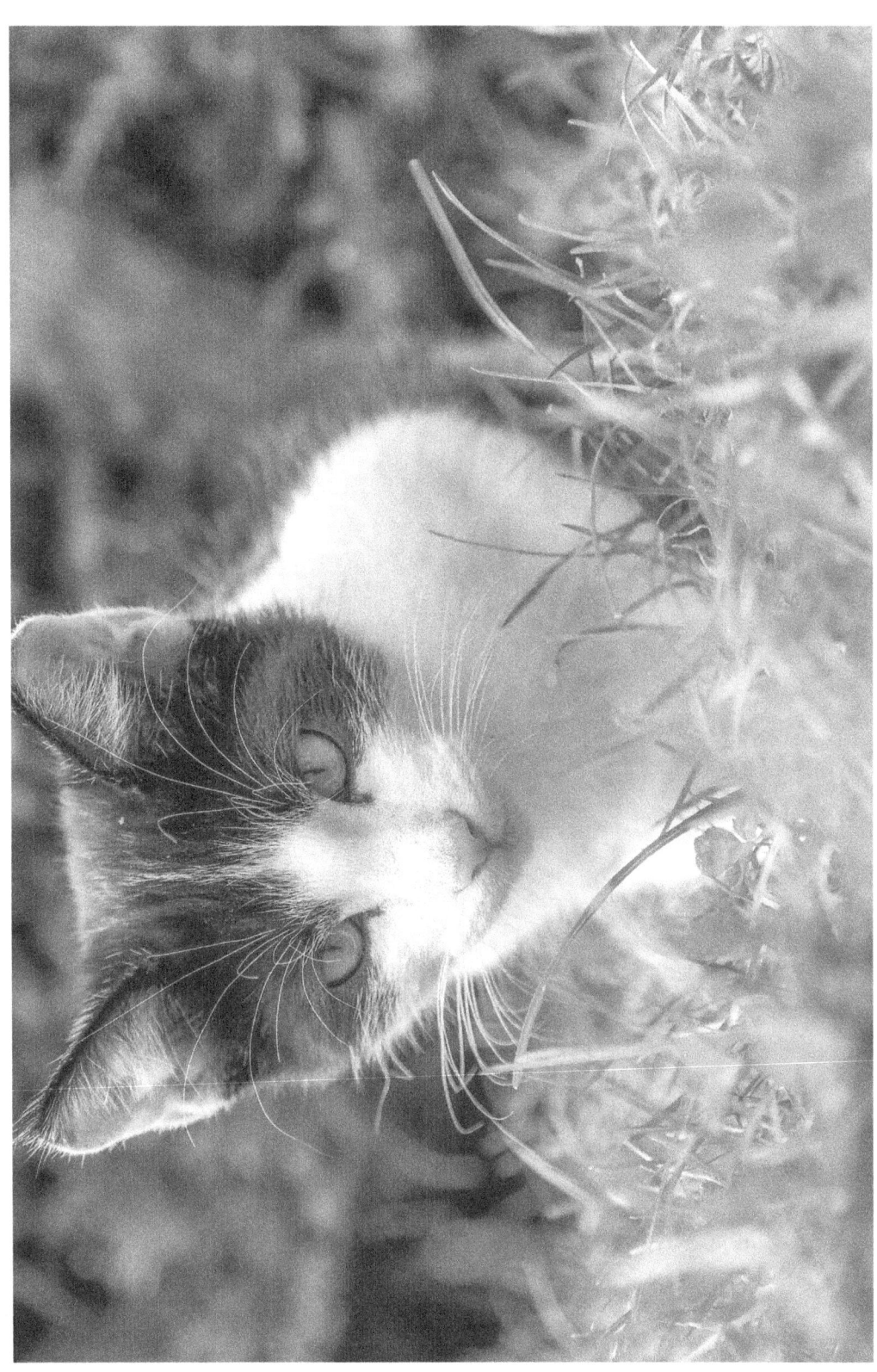

*"Kittens are wide-eyed, soft and sweet.
With needles in their jaws and feet."
~ Pam Brown*

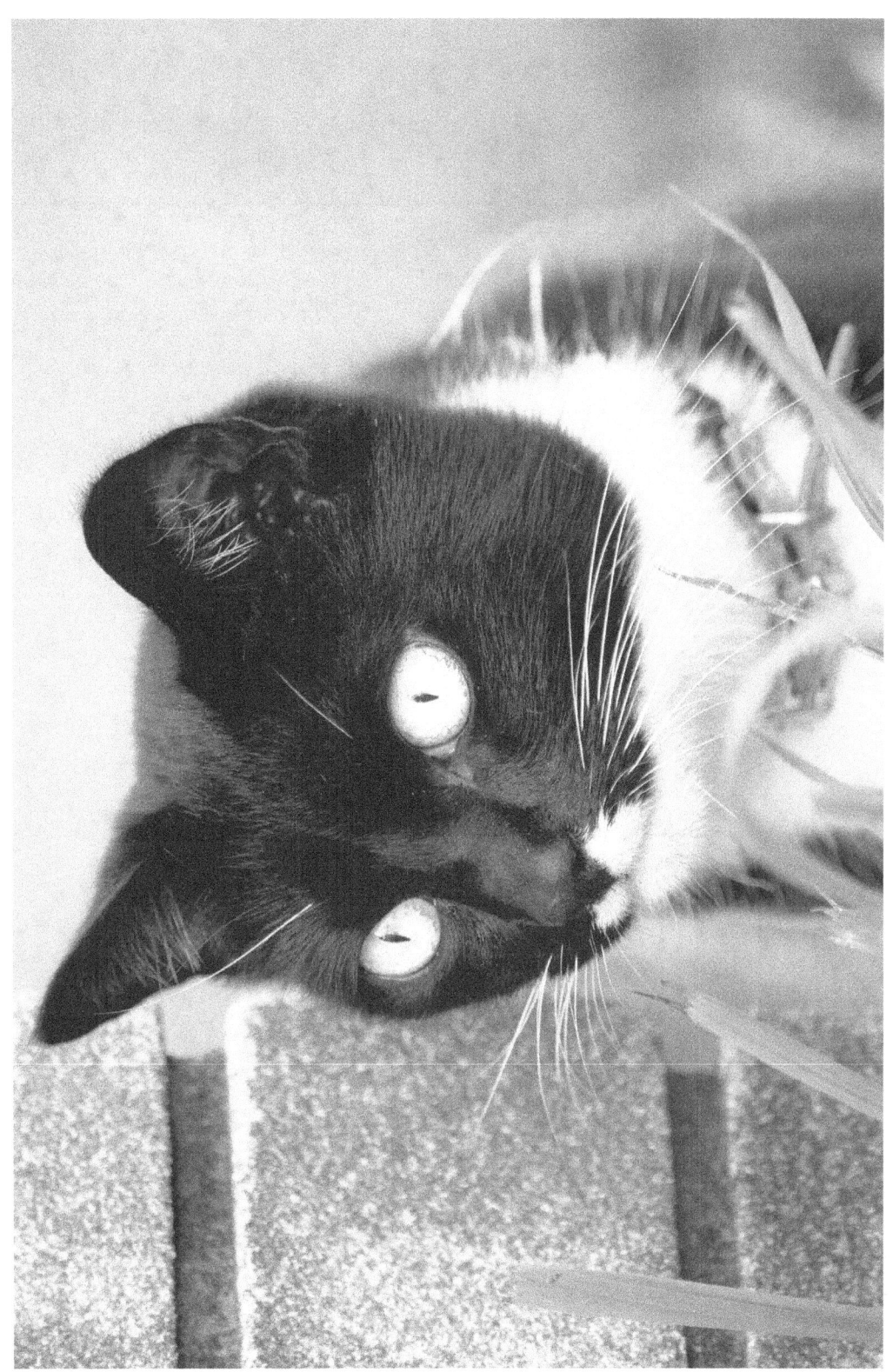

"The playful kitten, with its pretty little tigerish gambols, is infinitely more amusing than half the people one is obliged to live with in the world."
~ Lady Morgan Sydney

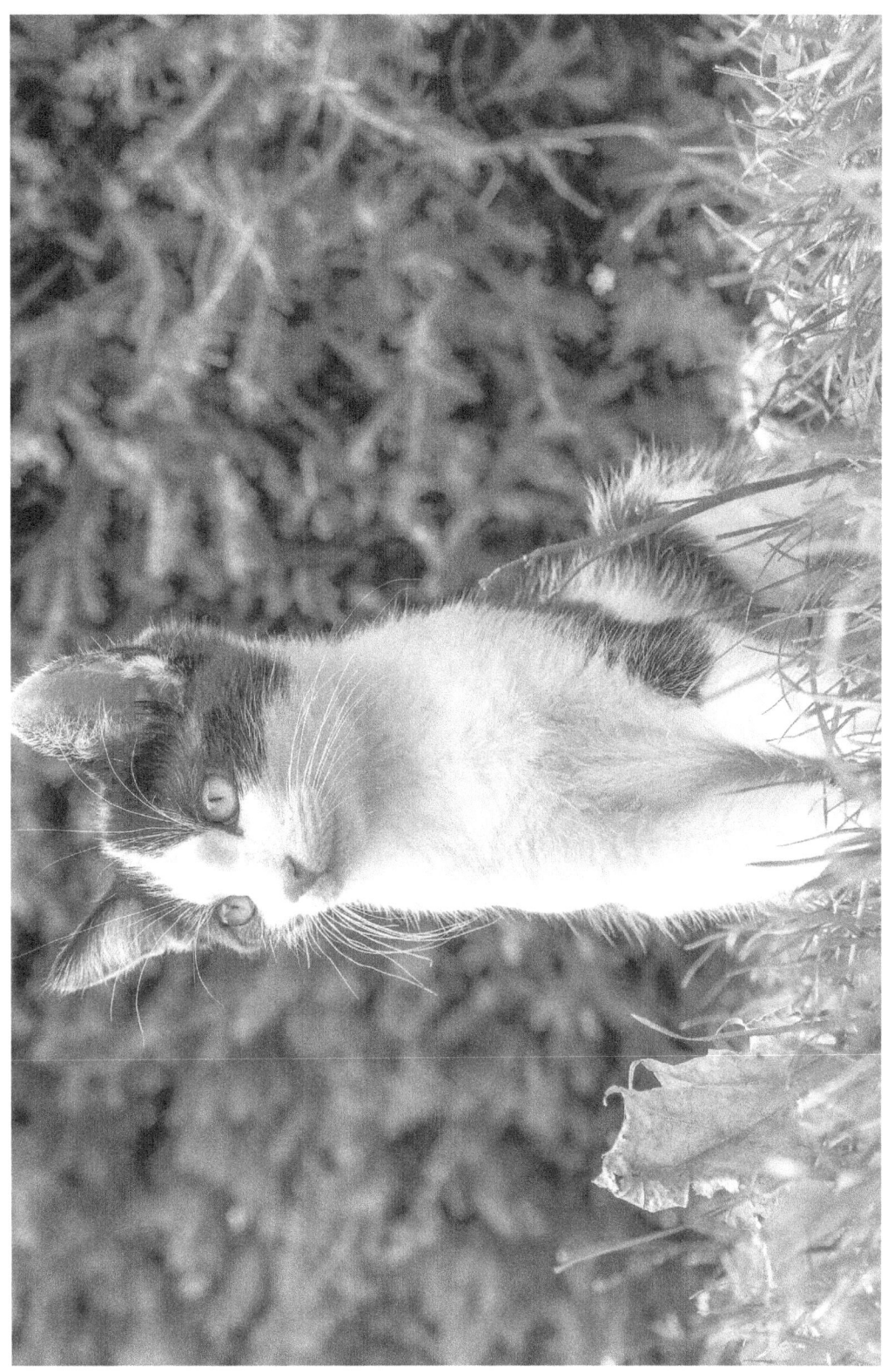

"Prowling his own quiet backyard or asleep by the fire, a kitten is still only a whisker away from the wilds."
~ Jean Burden

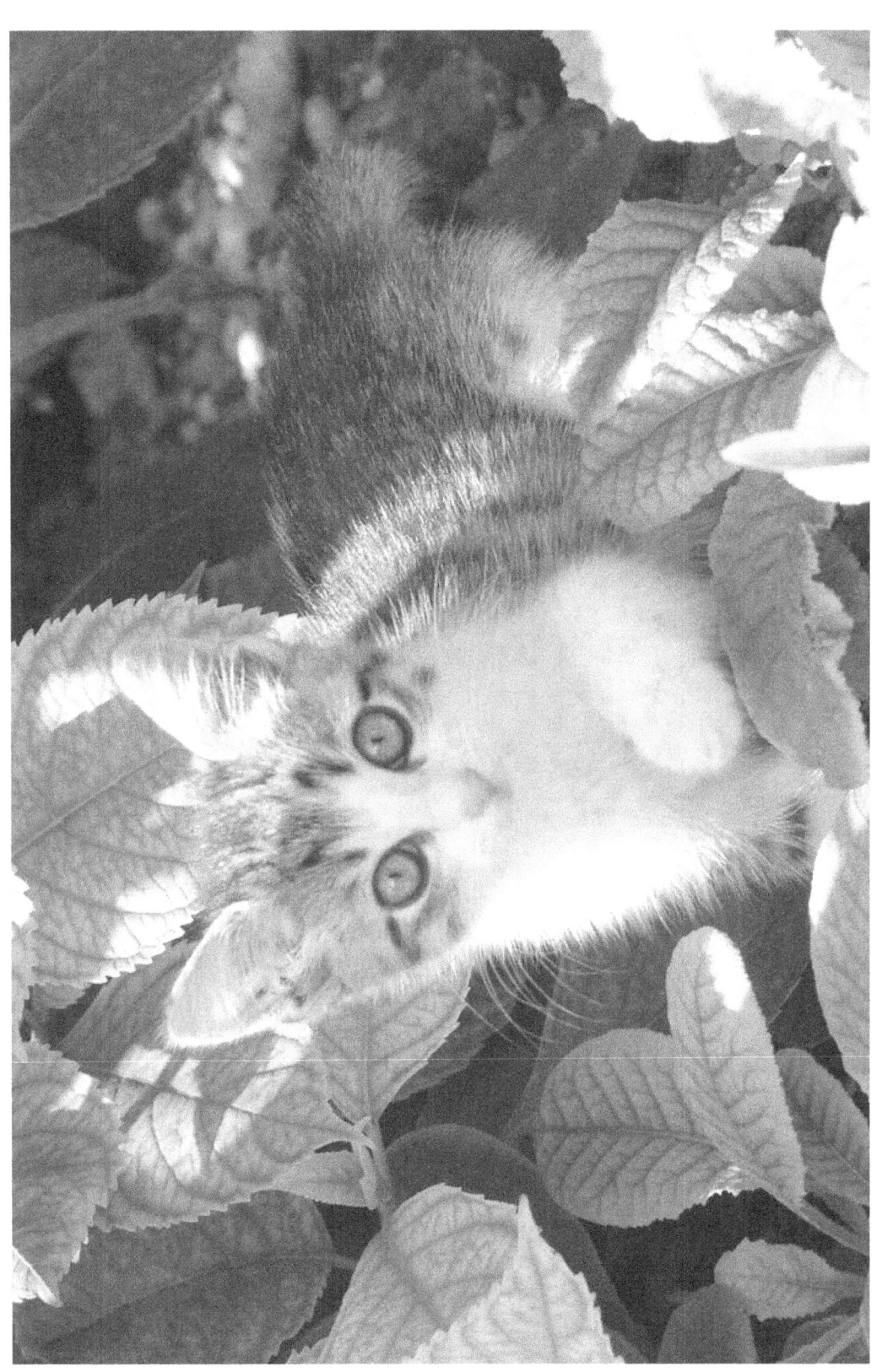

Kittens can happen to anyone.
   ~ Paul Gallico

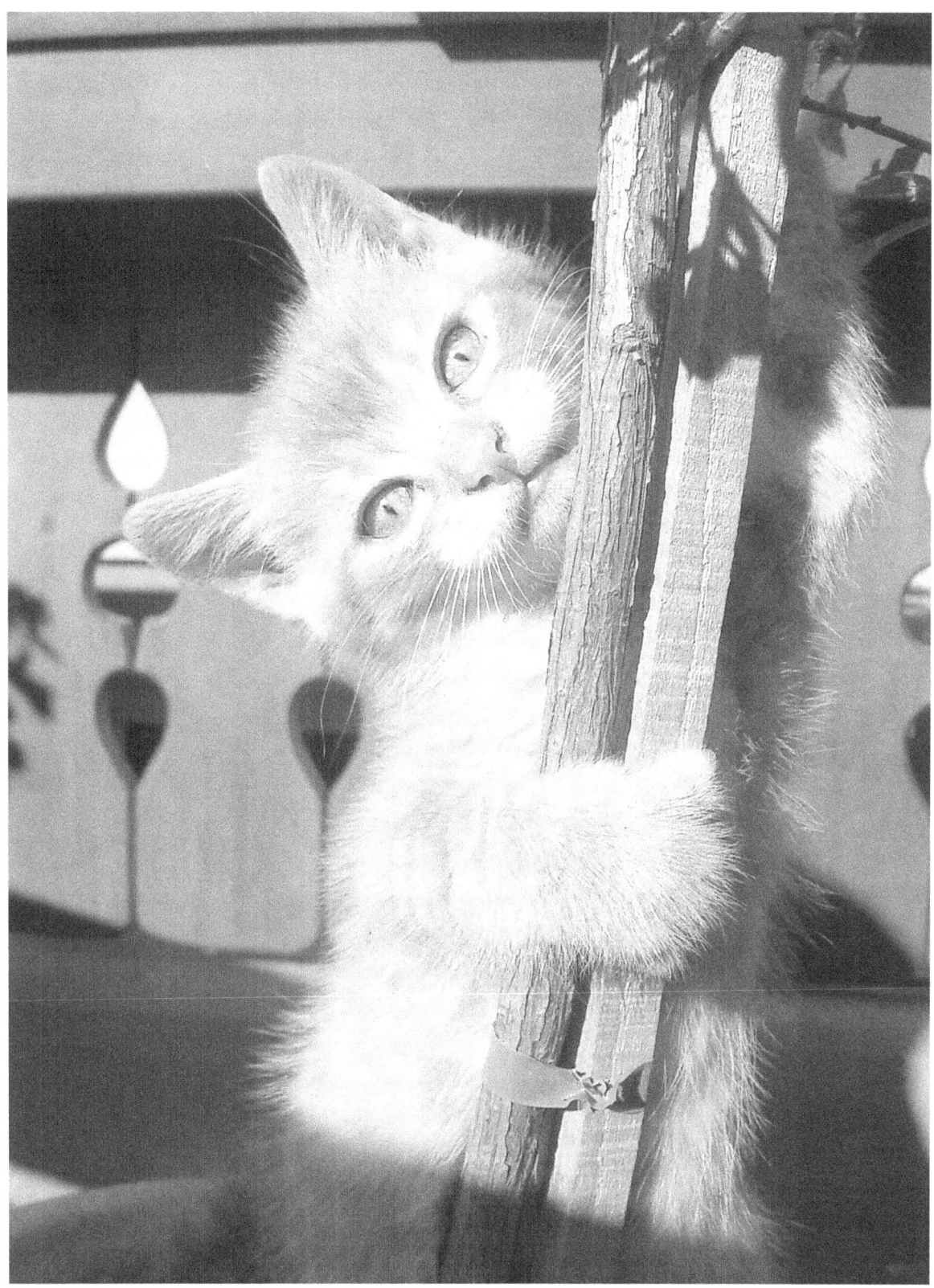

"It is impossible to keep a straight face in the presence of one or more kittens."
~ Cynthia E. Varnado

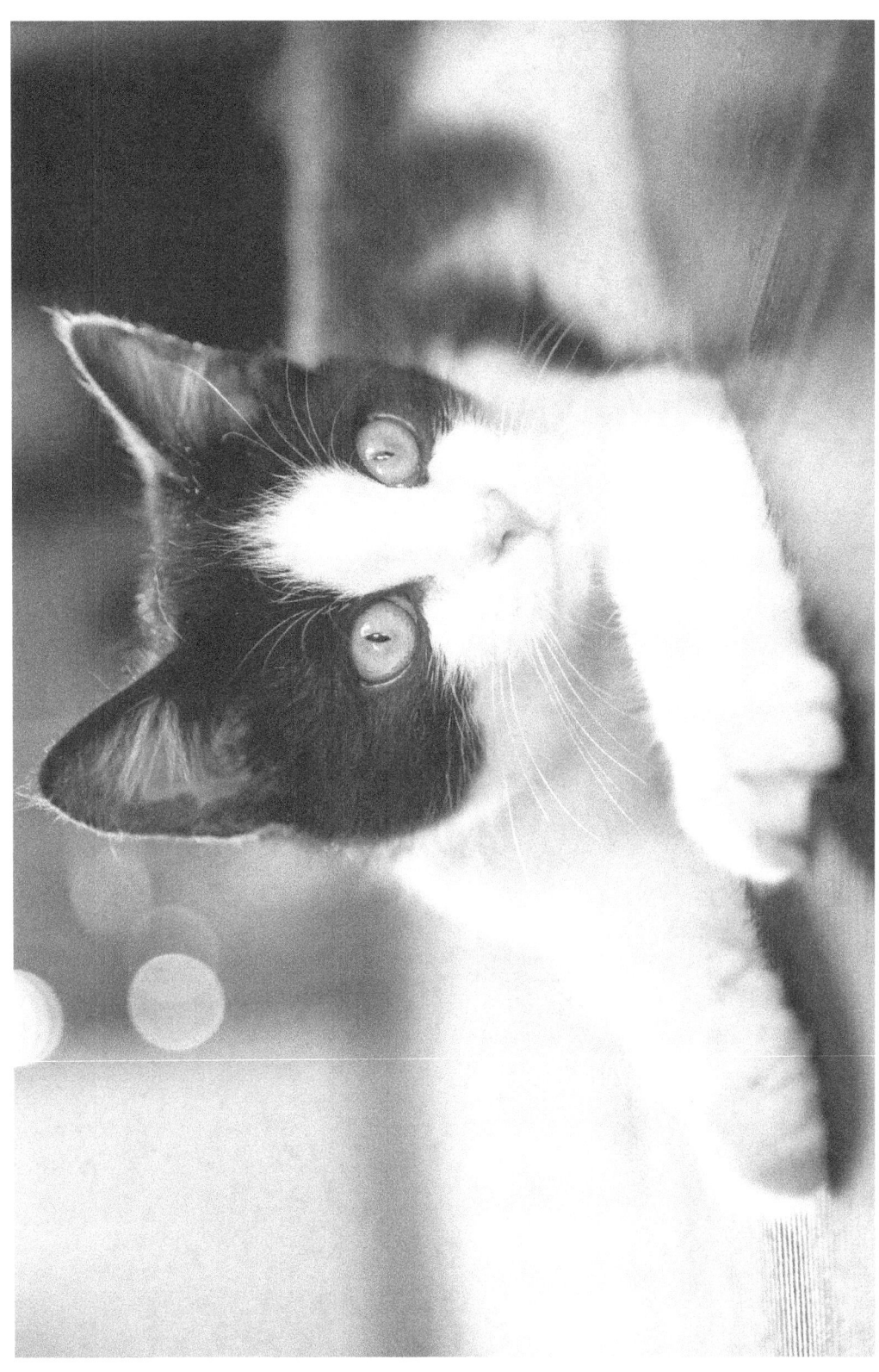

"But there was a kitten on my pillow, and it was purring in my face and vibrating gently with every purr, and, very soon, I slept."
~ Neil Gaiman

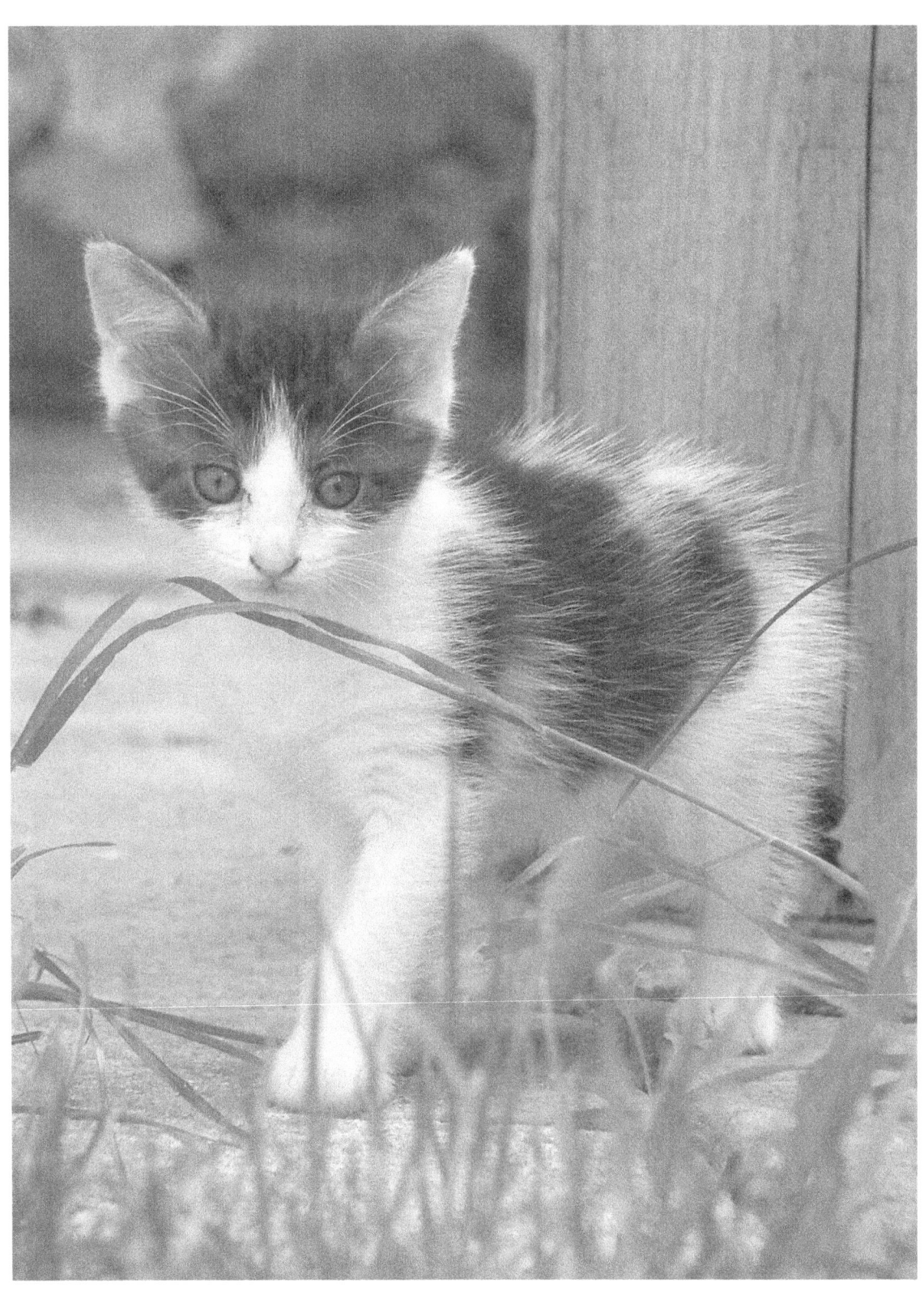

"A kitten is chiefly remarkable for rushing about like mad at nothing whatever, and generally stopping before it gets there."
~ Agnes Repplier

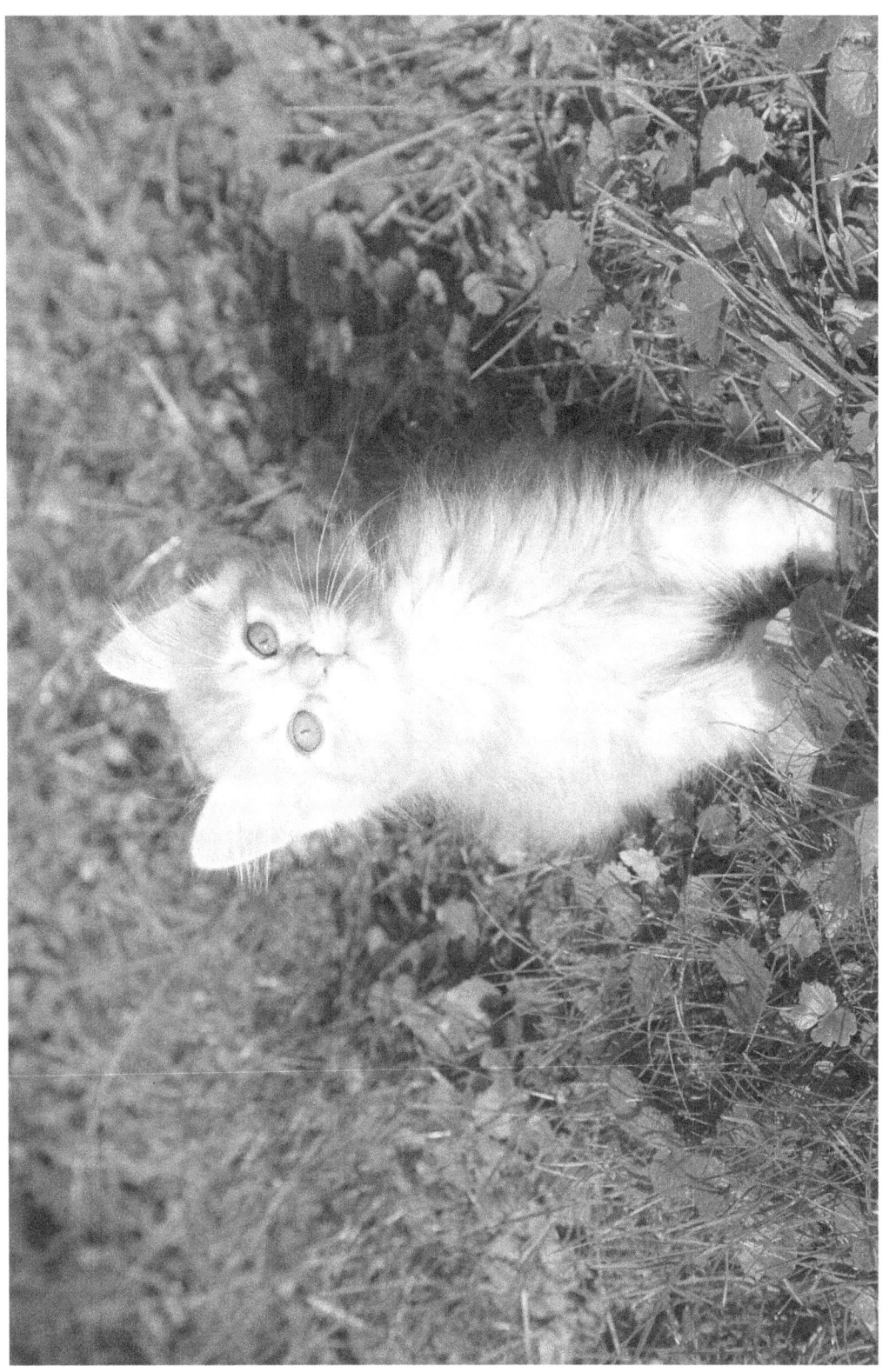

"The trouble with sharing one's bed with kittens is that they'd rather sleep on you than beside you."
~ Pam Brown

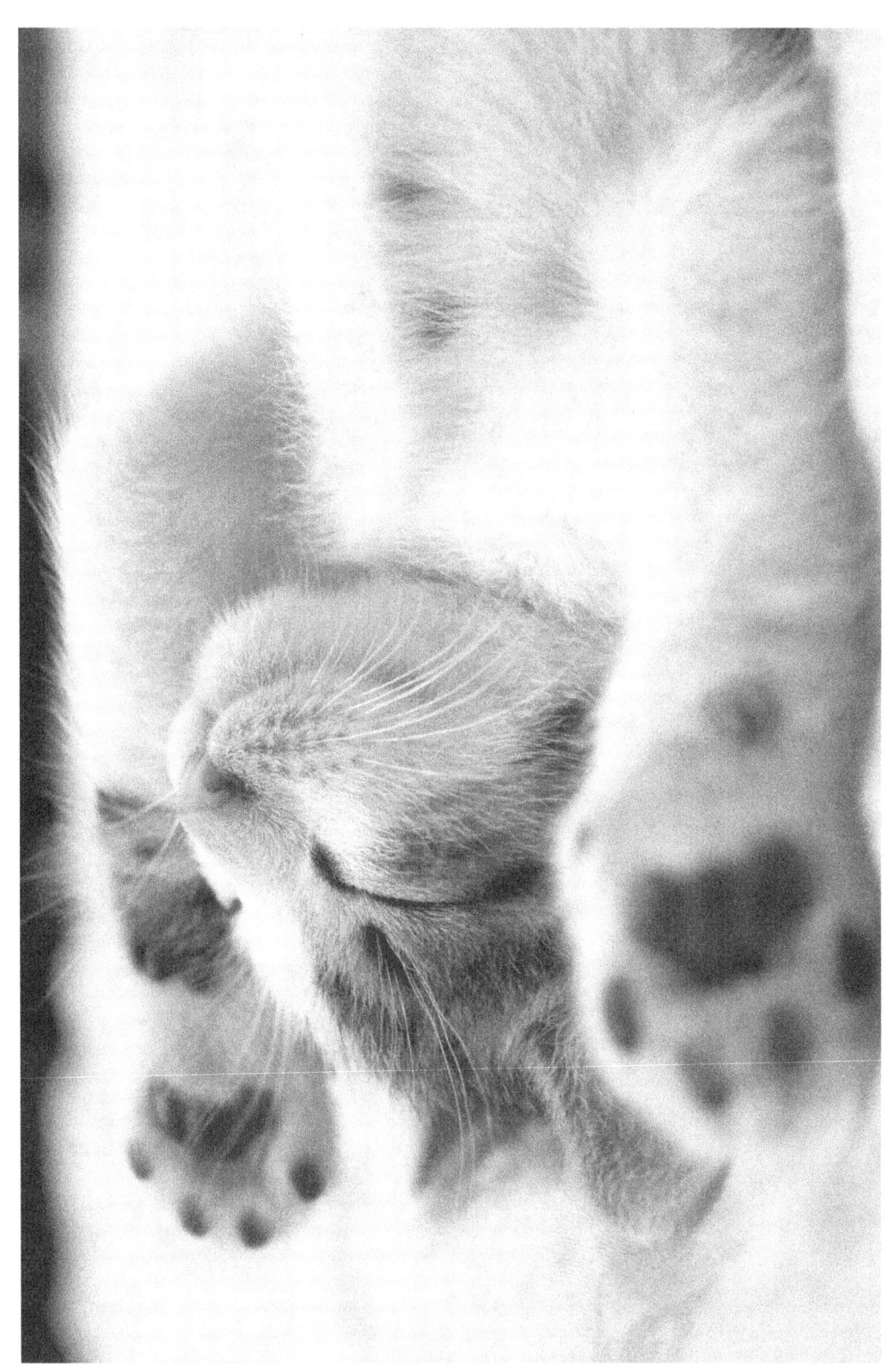

"Any kitten who misses a fly pretends it was aiming for the dead leaf."
~ Charlotte Gray

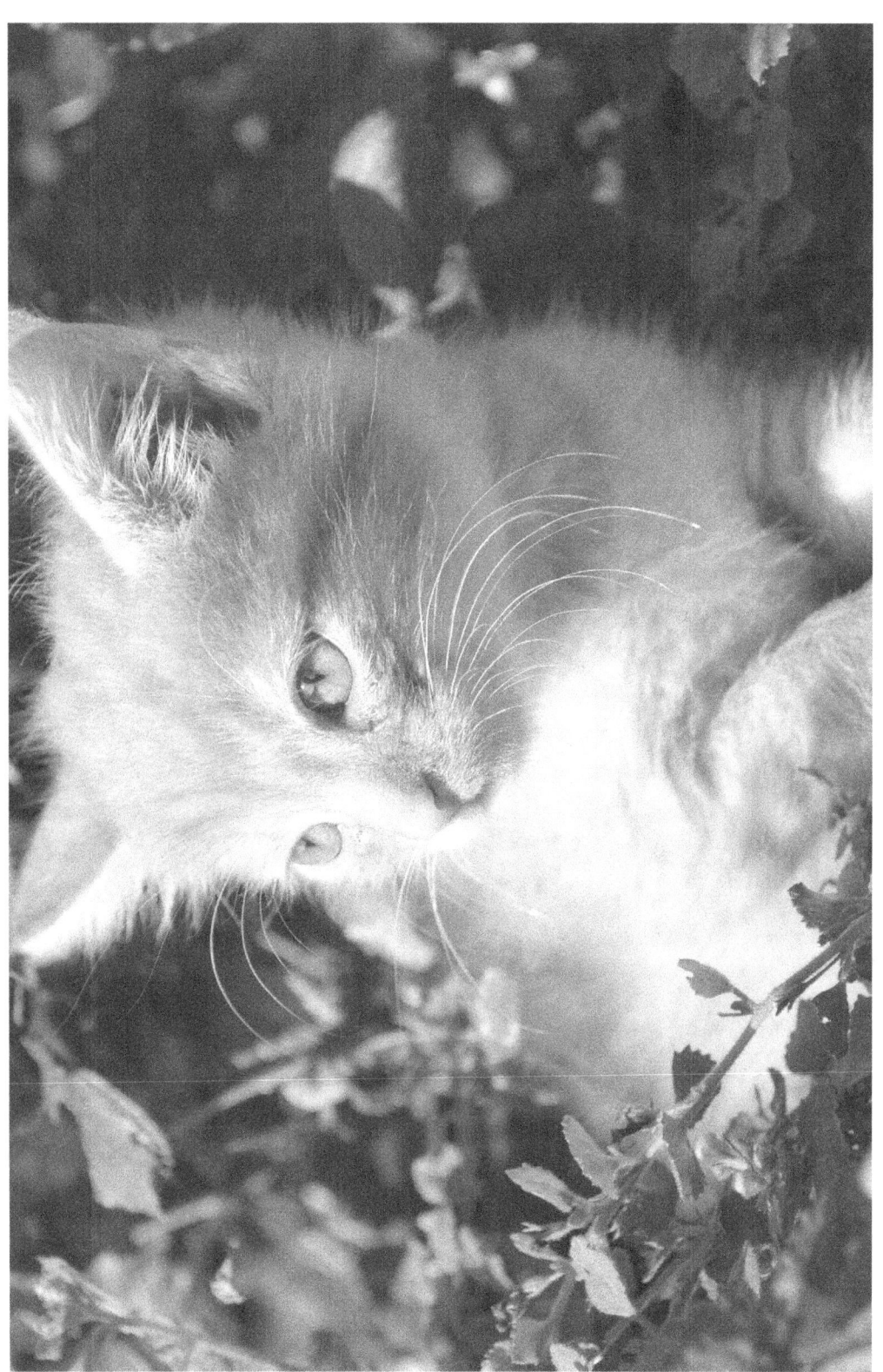

"There is something about the presence of a kitten... that seems to take the bite out of being alone."
~ Louis J. Camuti

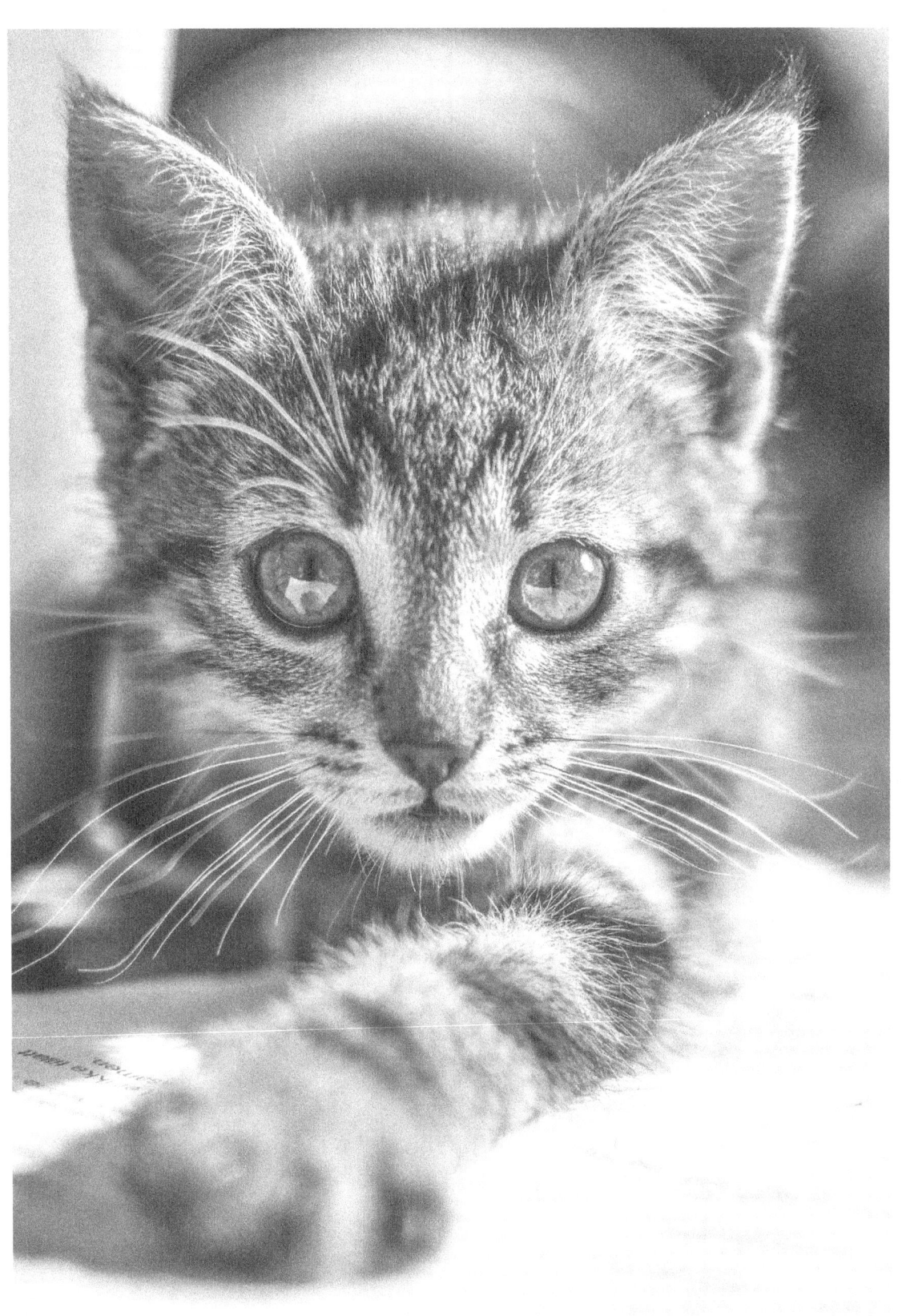

"Watch a kitten play for an hour and you will have tomes of wisdom to live a fun, courageous, and happy life."
~ Illyssa

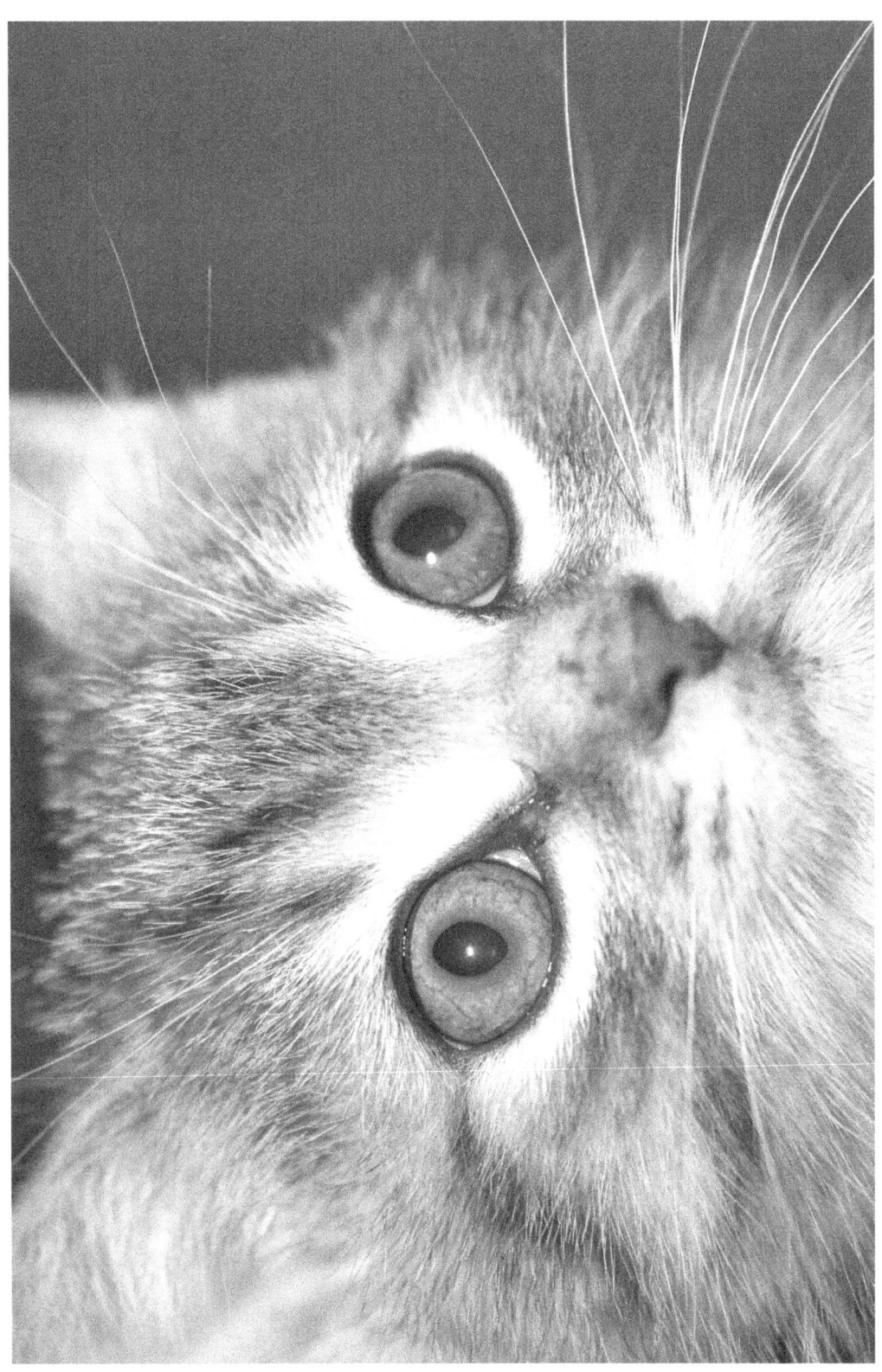

"Kittens are the only creatures that can be crazy without being institutionalized."
~ Jim Carey

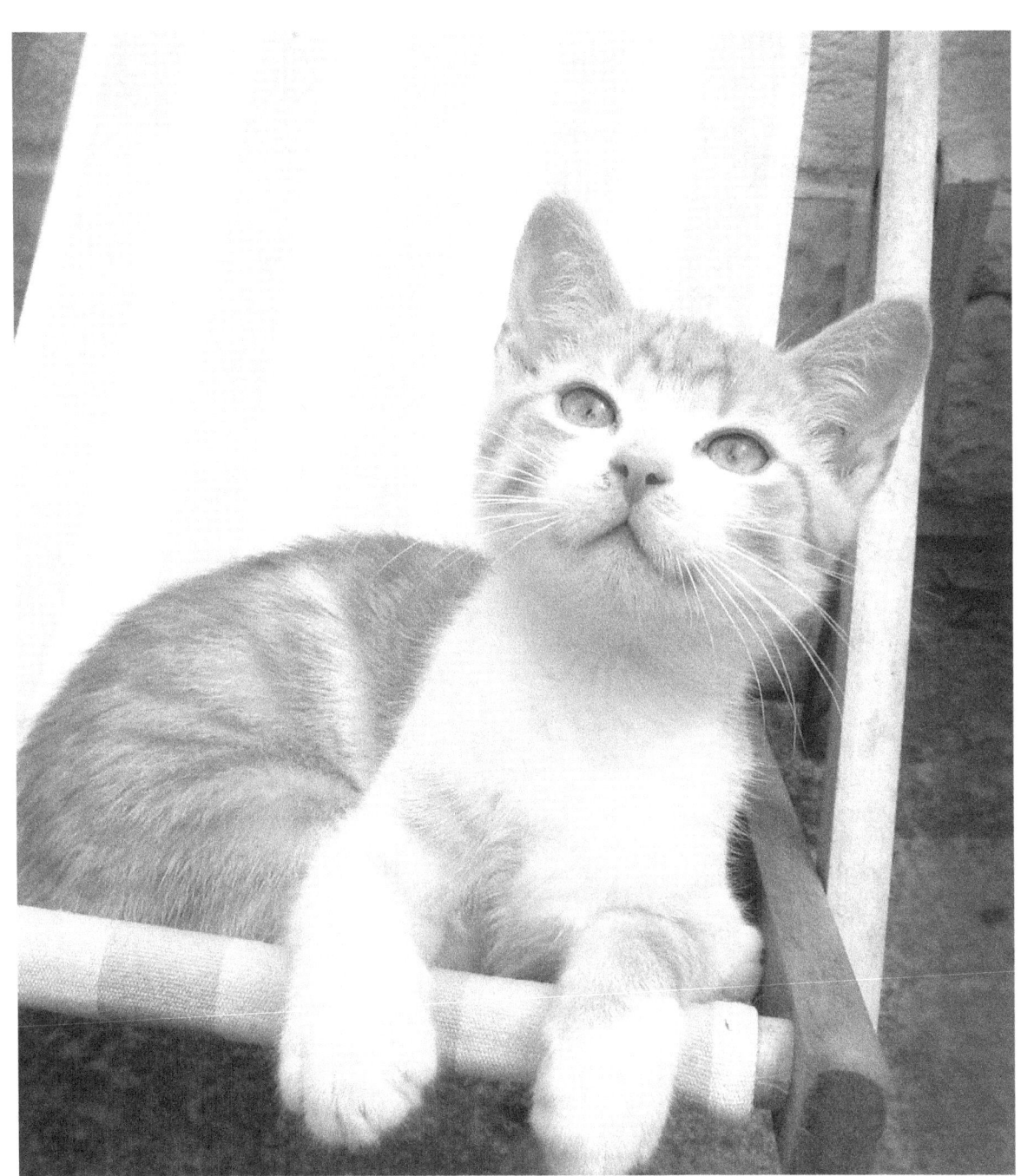

"A ball made of aluminum foil and a room full of kittens always fills a house with laughter."
~ Lucille Ball

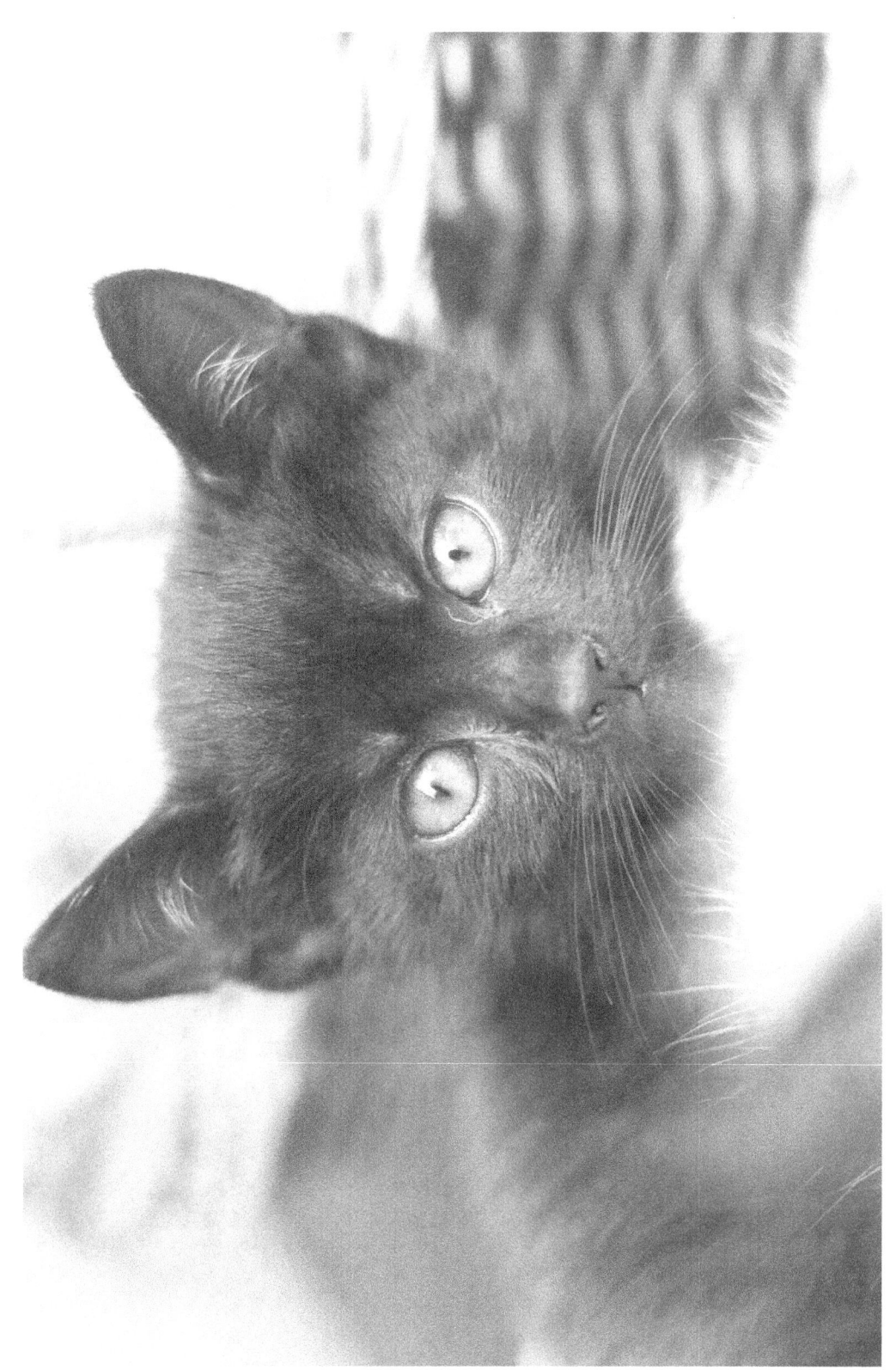

"Be like the curious kitten. Each minute is preoccupied with joy."
~ Chinese Proverb

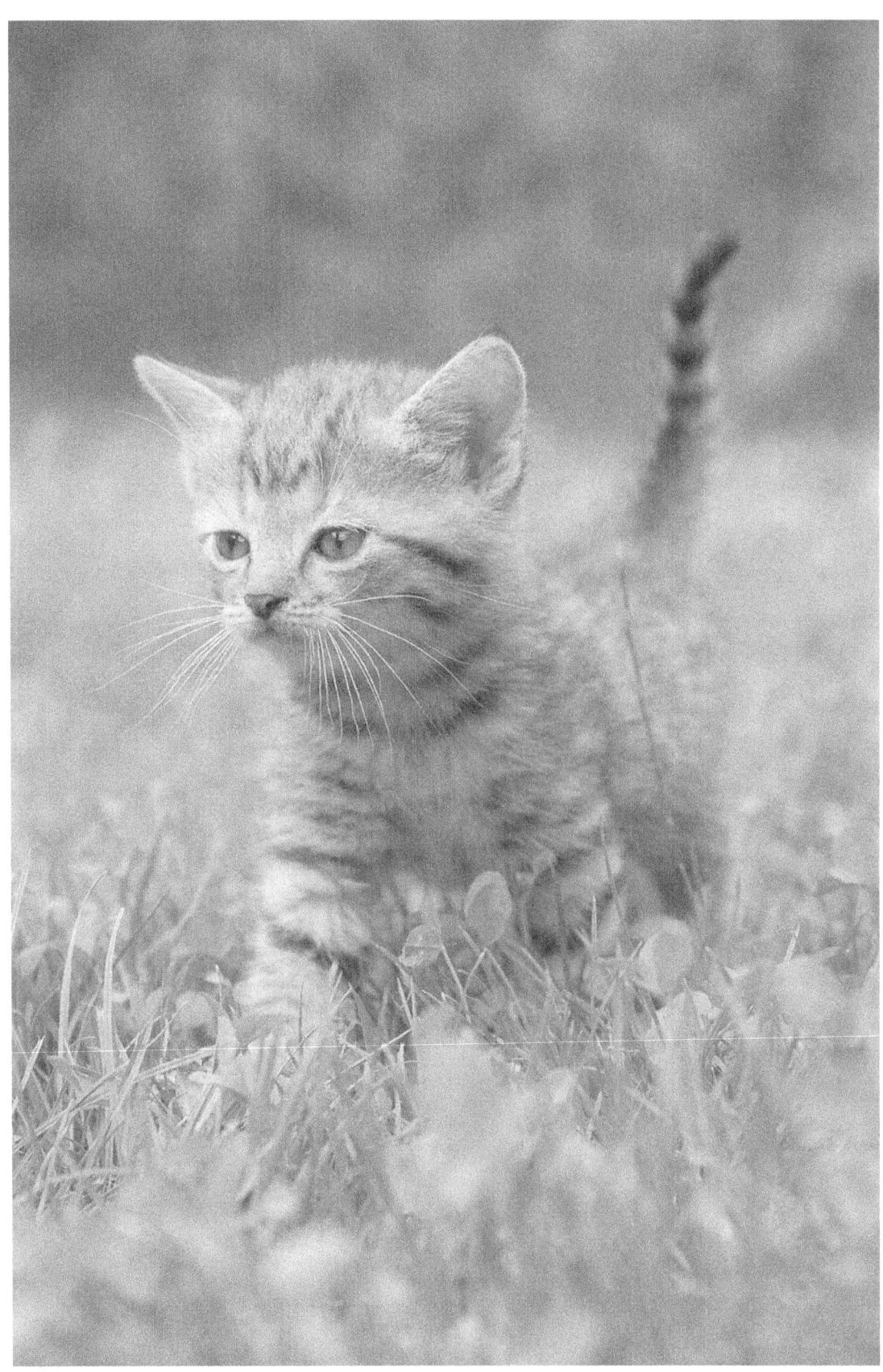

"My kitten speaks sign language with her tail." ~ Robert A. Stern

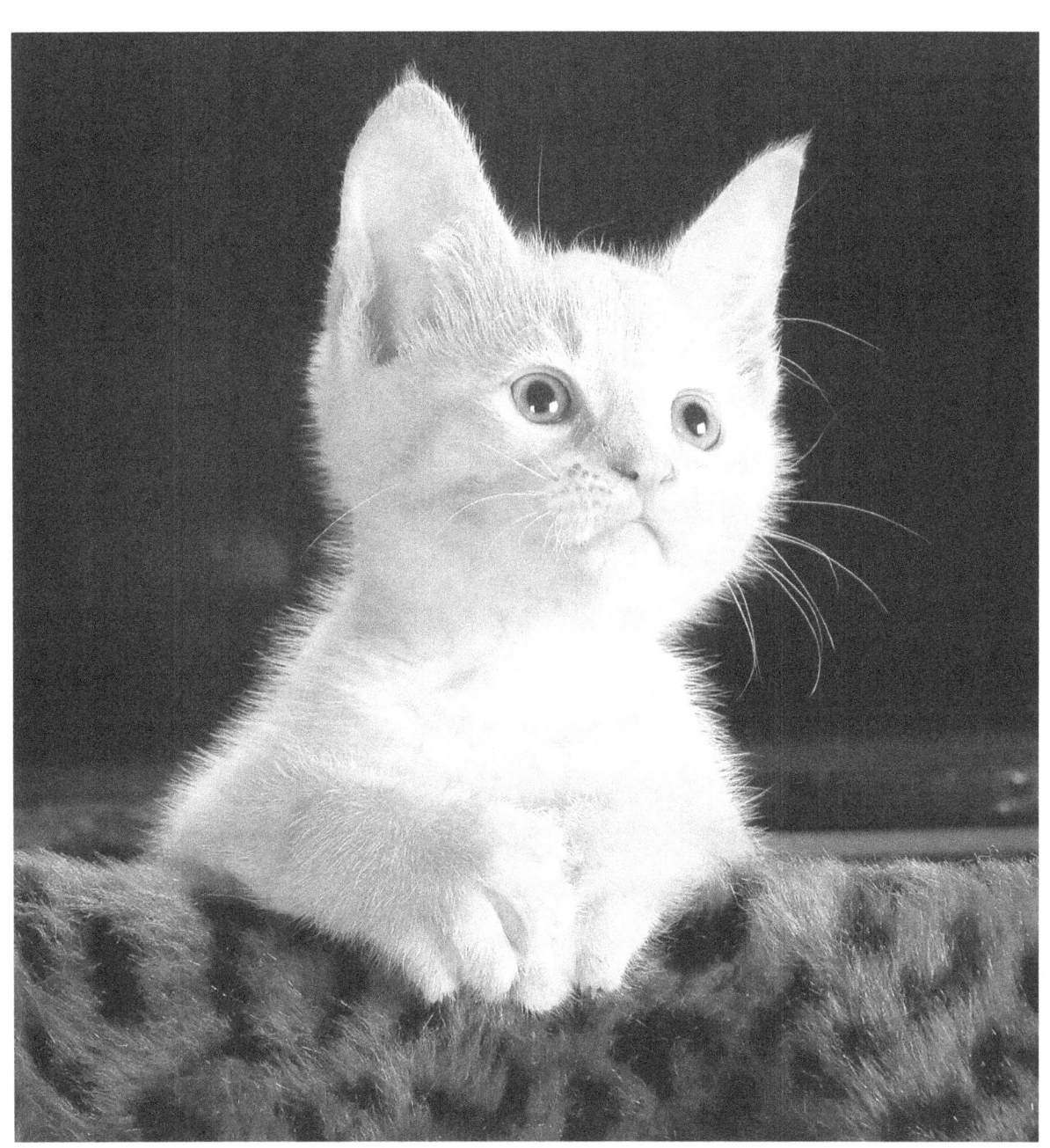

"Are we really sure the purring is coming from the kitty and not from our very own hearts?"
~ Terri Guillemets

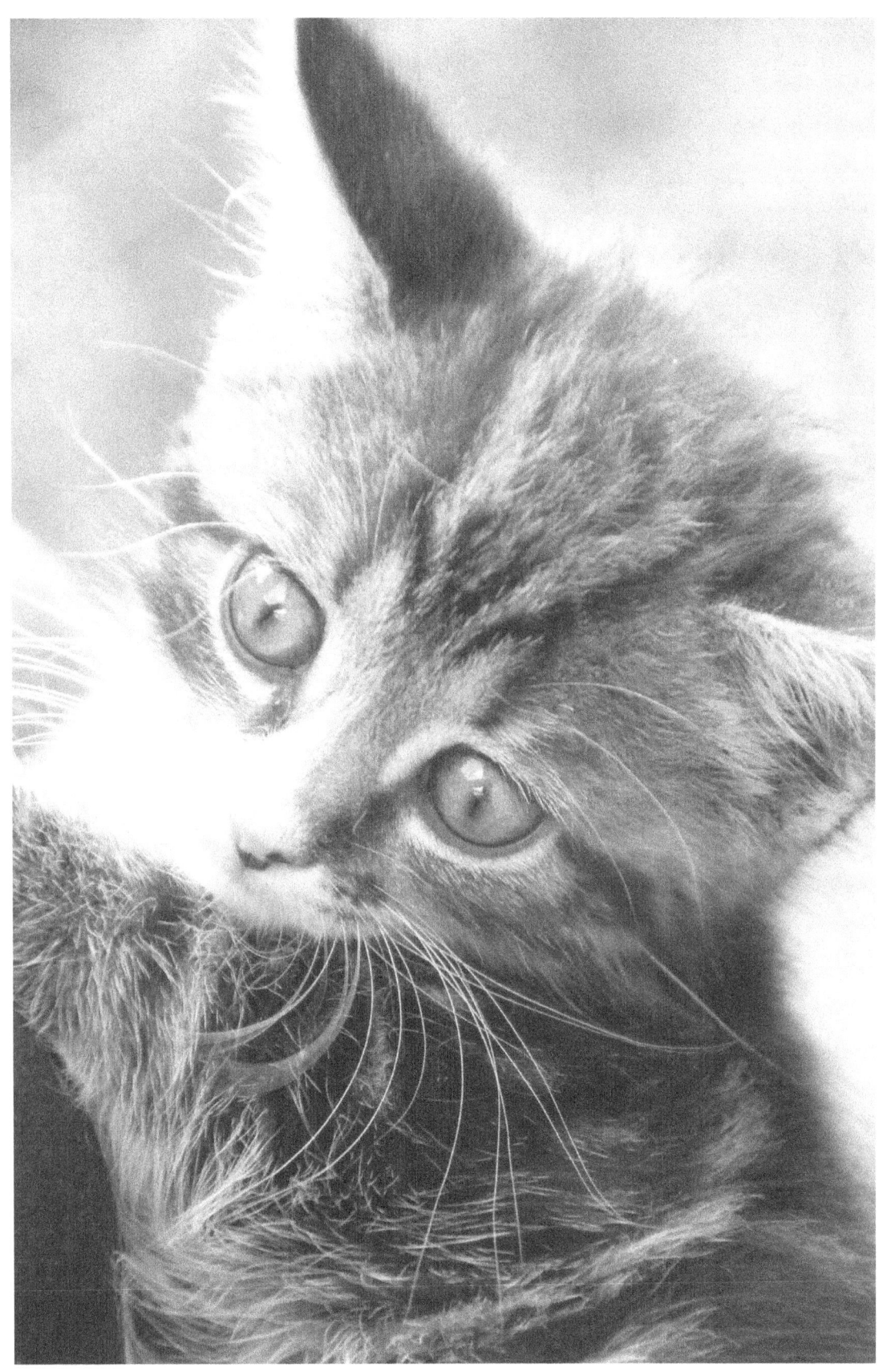